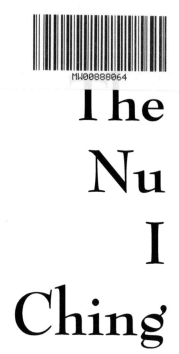

The
Nu
I
Ching

The Nu I Ching

a brief history predating King Wen
by 2000 years,
elucidating the ancient cryptogram

&

a three-tiered reading
using only one coin

Angelyn Ray

The Nu I Ching

a 3-tiered reading using one coin,
and a brief history predating King Wen by 2000 years
with an elucidation of the ancient cryptogram

by Angelyn Ray

copyright © 2008 by the author

Previous editions:
Yin Book of Change, by Murray Ray Brown © 1995
(Barbara Murray, the author, and Sharon Brown);
Ladybug I Ching, by the author as Sara Brown, © 1998;
The Easy I Ching © by the author, published 2005 by
The Aenor Trust, Salem, Oregon, USA.

ISBN: 1440455775

EAN-13: 9781440455773

Cover assembly: Moira Mann

Table of Contents
The Nu I Ching

To Shao Yung ~

who unearthed the ancient cryptogram
returning it to the light of heaven

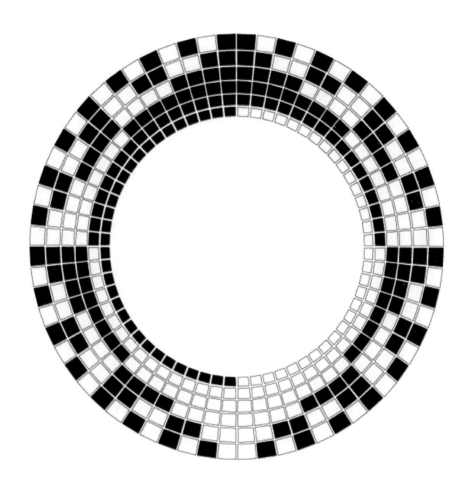

Figure 1
Ancient depiction of the 64 hexagrams

unknown origin
image courtesy of B. Pfennigschmidt

The Nu I Ching Oracle

Instructions

The Nu I Ching will illumine the concealed
aspects of your situation, including what you hold in your
own heart and mind, which may be vague or inaccessible
until you do the reading. Freely develop your own
approach and style with the oracle, and above all, enjoy
yourself. You will eventually form a direct resonance
with your inner pathways, and your reliance on the oracle
may diminish.

The Situation

"How to" questions work best, such as, "How can I
best approach (a given situation)?" "What do I need to
be aware of here?" Or just, "What about (a given
situation)?"

The Throw of the Coin

Hold a small coin between your palms while holding
your situation in mind. Shake and drop the coin six
times, recording each throw. The first throw becomes
Line 1 and is the bottom line. Line 6 will be the top line.

If "heads" is up, record a *single*, or *Yang*, line: ——

If "tails" is up, record an *open*, or *Yin*, line: — —

The Reading

Counting from the bottom line of your hexagram, find lines 3 and 4, the two middle lines. This is the "Heart" of your reading, which you will find between pages 10 and 13. As with our DNA codons, at the Heart level there are four possibilities.

After reading the Heart text, match the four middle lines of your hexagram to one of the four options shown at the end of your Heart reading. This is your "Mind" reading, which you will find between pages 14 and 29. As with our DNA codons, the four possibilities among the Heart hexagrams can be combined in four ways, offering sixteen possibilities at the Mind level (4x4=16).

When you have read the Mind text, match your hexagram to one of the four "Outer" hexagrams shown at the end of your Mind reading and found between pages 30 and 61. You are now proceeding from your inner resonance with the situation to the circumstances themselves as they manifest in your external reality. As with our DNA codons, at the Outer level there are 64 possibilities (4x4=16x4=64). The Outer hexagram completes your reading.

Usually the first reading is sufficient, but you may wish to address different aspects of the situation with more than one. Or the first answer may leave you with a new question that may be resolved by another reading. For example, if your reading recommends, "Bring heaven to earth now," and you are unclear as to how you may do this, you may want to ask, "How can I best bring heaven to earth now?" and throw the coin for another reading.

The Heart Hexagrams

0. Yin

— —
— —

You are the receptacle for strong creative force; you are not the force itself in this case. You are the bride, veiled at the wedding to the groom; you are the womb that holds the developing life in pristine conditions. Without you there will be no wedding; without you there will be no birth.

You are the pitcher that holds the milk and keeps it from spilling, the car that carries passengers to their destinations. You are the web that holds together all life, from the grains of sand on the beach to the planets and stars on their courses through the galaxies.

You are the principle of Divine Mother, guardian, nurturer, yet your innermost role is a strict and stringent one, for the mother must be ever vigilant or else her offspring dies, the guardian ever on guard; the nurturer must take care lest some poison enter the system.

Now find your Mind hexagram between pages 14-29
by matching your four middle lines:

0 Yin   1 Closure   32 Beginning   33 Nourishment

21. Becoming

Heart - the two middle lines of your hexagram

———
— —

    The situation for which you have consulted the I Ching comes out of a cycle of growth that has not yet reached its full potential. There is more to be gained, more blossom to come to fruit, more fish to fry, pertaining to your inner development in the matter at hand. You would be wise to pay attention to nurturing the needs of your spirit, to meditation, artistic pursuit, music, aromatherapy, to greater familiarity with the earth and with beauty of all kinds.

    It is essential that you value each separate step of this journey as you value life itself, for it is your life. Nature and beauty will lead you into the paths that will bring you to the completion of this phase, when *becoming* becomes *being*, a finished work of the spirit.

*Now find your Mind hexagram between pages 14-29
by matching your four middle lines:*

10 Inquiry   11 Growth   42 Being   43 Wholeness

42. Being

Heart - the two middle lines of your hexagram

— —
———

The situation for which you have consulted the I Ching comes out of a grounded, matured cycle of growth. Once ground is gained and maturity is achieved, the inner growth has peaked. It is time to move on to a new phase of learning. In effect, you have graduated; you have won, or are winning, the awards for your efforts. You have brought into being some reality for which you have labored.

Once a lesson is learned, a thing achieved, it is done; completed. You may enjoy it for a time, but to tarry overlong would be to invite stagnation. It stands now on its own in history, recorded or not, and you, the learner and creator, are about to move on to new discoveries, new learning, new becoming. This is how you move along with the universe on its course of freedom.

Now find your Mind hexagram between pages 14-29 by matching your four middle lines:

20 Acquittal 21 Becoming 52 Repose 53 Differentiation

63. Yang

Heart - the two middle lines of your hexagram

―――――
―――――

You are the star that lights the way and gives direction to the navigator. You are the seed sown in the earth, the pattern that determines the form life is to assume. You are the groom at the wedding, the seed sown in the womb. You give life because you are life; you make love because you are love.

You are the singer and the songwriter, the artist and the artist's tools. You are the milk in the pitcher, the water in the well, the captain of the ship. Without you all vessels would remain empty, all skies without stars, all seas without life. At your central core is the impetus for life and the substance of all dreams.

You are the principle of Divine Father, guide and sustainer, and your innermost role calls for the utmost in empathy, compassion, and mercy.

Now find your Mind hexagram between pages 14-29 by matching your four middle lines:

30 Anticipation   31 Sustaining   62 Change   63 Yang

The Mind Hexagrams

0. Yin

Your four center lines are:

‍ ‍ ‍ ‍ ‍ ‍ ‍ ‍ ‍ ‍ ‍ ‍ ‍ ‍ — —
‍ ‍ ‍ ‍ ‍ ‍ ‍ ‍ ‍ ‍ ‍ ‍ ‍ ‍ — —
‍ ‍ ‍ ‍ ‍ ‍ ‍ ‍ ‍ ‍ ‍ ‍ ‍ ‍ — —
‍ ‍ ‍ ‍ ‍ ‍ ‍ ‍ ‍ ‍ ‍ ‍ ‍ ‍ — —

It is up to you to provide the impetus for action on the part of others. You are not the principal character in the current situation, but without you no principal character will act.

Be crystal clear, and communicate with others with laser-like insight, impelled by uncompromising will and desire. You are to provide shape to the situation for which you have consulted the I Ching as the womb severely constrains the babe.

Now find your Outer hexagram between pages 30-61 by matching the hexagram:

0 Yin   1 Closure   32 Beginning   33 Nourishment

1. Closure
Mind

Your four center lines are:

```
 ___  ___
 ___  ___
 _ _  _ _
 _ _  _ _
```

It is time to draw to a close some key aspect of the situation for which you have consulted the I Ching.

Perhaps closure is occurring without your design. If this is the case, you will soon understand the wisdom of it, because from a higher perspective this closure comes in the natural flow.

Graciously turn your attention inward, to taking inventory, finishing, and wrapping things up in your own mind, in your own order. Your actions will then reflect the balance and centering you so achieve.

Now find your Outer hexagram between pages 30-61
by matching the hexagram:

2 Connection   3 Centering   34 Birth 35 Compassion

10. Inquiry
Mind

Your four center lines are:

$$\equiv\equiv$$

The situation for which you have consulted the I Ching has led you a complicated way. It is not over.

You have been challenged, tested, and brought under critical scrutiny. You have been pushed into areas of experience that have brought discomfort and dismay, yet in enduring them and coming this far, you have gained the opportunity to achieve inner growth beyond your greatest hopes. Be thankful for this.

You have not lost, rather you have profited, exchanging shallowness for depth and compassion.

Now find your Outer hexagram between pages 30-61
by matching the hexagram:

4 Attunement   5 Opening   36 Induction   37 Endurance

11. Growth
Mind

Your four center lines are:

There is a burgeoning development in the situation for which you have consulted the I Ching. It has not yet reached its peak.

It is important that you focus on your own inner growth at this time and not on managing or controlling the flow of circumstance, which has already been set in motion. Any needed control on your part will flow naturally and easily into place with others involved in the situation.

'Coincidences' - synchronicities - will impel you to bring to bear your wisdom and skills.

Now find your Outer hexagram between pages 30-61 by matching the hexagram:

6 Alliance   7 Patience 38 Balance   39 Spontaneity

20. Acquittal
Mind

Your four center lines are:

```
—   —
— — —
—   —
```

You are without blame in the situation for which you have consulted the I Ching. You have conducted yourself in the most befitting manner at each turn.

The nature of your next cycle of growth is up to you. You need not push through or rush things along now. Take your time, trusting in the power that has led you this far, that is with you in rest, and that will lead you again.

Now find your Outer hexagram between pages 30-61
by matching the hexagram:

8 Innocence   9 Reflection   40 Paradox   41 Benediction

21. Becoming
Mind

Your four center lines are:

```
―― ―
― ――
―― ―
―  ―
```

The situation for which you have consulted the I Ching entails a process that is leading you toward some tangible achievement, which represents the completion of a major cycle of growth for you.

Whether or not the project succeeds, your progress need not be deterred.

Whatever you are becoming in the world of created manifestations, it is what your spirit is becoming in the spirit realm that counts, and in the long run, only this.

Now find your Outer hexagram between pages 30-61 by matching the hexagram:

10 Inquiry   11 Growth   42 Being   43 Wholeness

30. Anticipation
Mind

Your four center lines are:

— —
————
————
— —

     Enjoy this time of anticipation regarding the situation for which you have consulted the I Ching. Your current path may not seem to be sustaining but the destiny will prove that it was.

     As things stand now, they represent the lull between highs, the gap between situations in which you feel more comfortable and in control. These lulls and gaps are crucially important to your inner development.

     Find comfort within while in the situation just as it is. Willing to let go control, you prepare effectively for later action.

Now find your Outer hexagram between pages 30-61
by matching the hexagram:

12 Recognition 13 Fortuity 44 Epiphany 45 Combustion

31. Sustaining
Mind

Your four center lines are:

$$\begin{array}{c} \rule{2em}{0.1em} \\ \rule{2em}{0.1em} \\ \rule{2em}{0.1em} \\ \rule{0.8em}{0.1em}\ \rule{0.8em}{0.1em} \end{array}$$

In order to keep abreast of the constant current of change in the situation for which you have consulted the I Ching, you are now called upon to adapt to a given set of circumstances.

You are faced with the paradox: Remain unchanging in order to effect the changes you want.

By settling in and becoming secure in things just as they are, you will be able to transcend the bonds that restrain you.

Now find your Outer hexagram between pages 30-61 by matching the hexagram:

14 Affinity 15 Equilibrium 46Momentum 47Networking

32. Beginning
Mind

Your four center lines are:

$$\equiv\ \ \equiv$$

    The circumstances for which you have consulted the I Ching hold the possibility of a new era for you, in which you are the vehicle for something great. The potential at this time is limitless. The opportunity now present has far-reaching implications.

    What do you want to accomplish? The greatest gain will come out of your bringing to bear all the wisdom from all the lessons you have ever learned. The challenge is enormous, but the result will be well worth the discipline required.

Now find your Outer hexagram between pages 30-61
by matching the hexagram:

16 Inclusion   17 Questing 48 Awareness   49 Simplicity

33. <u>Nourishment</u>

Mind

Your four center lines are:

―――
― ―
― ―
―――

The situation for which you have consulted the I Ching is one in which you are provided with vital sustenance for your heart and spirit. By being so nurtured you are becoming the nurturer.

Take the time now to savor the spiritual banquet just for the experience itself. Although it prepares you for greater service as a nurturer, the point now is to be the recipient.

Play well the role of the receiver of gifts as if this is all there is because for now, it is.

Now find your Outer hexagram between pages 30-61
by matching the hexagram:

18 Immersion   19 Healing   50 Definition   51 Deepening

42. Being
Mind

Your four center lines are:

```
— —
— —
— —
———
```

You have achieved measurable progress in the situation for which you have consulted the I Ching.

You have in fact come so far as to warrant some celebration. Mark your accomplishment with something tangible: a card, a letter or gift sent, a special symbolic item gathered, or a worldwide party!

At the mountaintop, relax and enjoy the view before you start down the other side, ready to proceed to the next mountain.

Now find your Outer hexagram between pages 30-61 by matching the hexagram:

20 Acquittal 21 Becoming   52 Repose 53Differentiation

43. Wholeness
Mind

Your four center lines are:

You are challenged to become part of a much greater whole in the situation for which you have consulted the I Ching. The challenge lies in the extent of your readiness to give up the need to be your own pet.

Pettiness dissolves in the glow of universal gain as the mist dissolves in the sun.

The sacrifice of the small self is no sacrifice at all when what you stand to win is the universe! And you do stand to win it. So give in. Go with the flow and become the flow.

Now find your Outer hexagram between pages 30-61 by matching the hexagram:

22 Humility   23 Pause   54 Devotion   55 Equality

52. Repose
Mind

Your four center lines are:

```
 ═   ═
 ═══════
 ═══════
```

   You are on your way to the stars. Rest assured and drink deeply of the nectar for which you have long toiled. You have surmounted the obstacles put in your way and thrown off the dead weight of outgrown worth. This is no small accomplishment.

   The situation for which you have consulted the I Ching is far more than a reward. It is the result of lifetimes of directed focus, and it is your invitation to enter an entirely new way of being.

Now find your Outer hexagram between pages 30-61
by matching the hexagram:

24Determination 25Recovery 56Oneness 57Sensitivity

53. Differentiation
Mind

Your four center lines are:

```
_____  _  _
_  _  _  _
_____
_____
```

In order to complete the issue concerning the situation for which you have consulted the I Ching, it is essential that you recognize and accept your individual uniqueness, which is your Holy Grail, your Ex Calibur.

Without realizing your uniqueness and allowing its full manifestation, you are bound to wander in the mists of the lowlands.

Come to terms with the challenge of freeing your spirit and the opportunity to enter realities untold is yours.

Now find your Outer hexagram between pages 30-61 by matching the hexagram:

26 Honor   27 Submission 58 Attention 59 Expansion

62. Change
Mind

Your four center lines are:

```
 _   _
 _____
 _____
```

The motivation for change in the current situation depends on you. You are in the driver's seat; you handle the controls which may bring about the needed changes. And change *is* needed, for you have outgrown the familiar circumstances.

In order to move along in development you must enter the paradox: Conform to the demand for change. Catch up to it and keep up with it.

Now find your Outer hexagram between pages 30-61 by matching the hexagram:

28 Constancy 29 Inspiration 60 Charisma 61 Bounty

63. Yang

Mind

Your four center lines are:

You are the spearhead in the current situation. Any action to be taken is up to you. You hold the power to decide the way things go, the direction they will flow.

It is essential that you act, and that you do so with all mercy. Not only do these circumstances depend on your being motivated by mercy, your own development depends on it. Mercy is at the heart of the true character of Yang.

Now find your Outer hexagram between pages 30-61 by matching the hexagram:

30 Anticipation 31 Sustaining 62 Change   63 Yang

The Outer Hexagrams

0. Yin

Mind: 0 Yin
Heart: 0 Yin

Trigrams: Earth comes into Earth

What dream is in the dark earth, waiting to be born?
It is yours to determine.
It is yours to bring forth.

1. Closure

Mind: 0 Yin
Heart: 0 Yin

Trigrams: Earth comes into Mountain

See the greater overtake the lesser.
Feel loss bring the promise of the new.
Release the old and welcome the new.

2. Connection

Mind: 1 Closure
Heart: 0 Yin

Trigrams: Earth comes into Water

```
== ==
== ==
== ==
```

New connections bring new horizons.
For complete connection include all four realms:
Physical, intellectual, emotional, and spiritual.

3. Centering

Mind: 1 Closure
Heart: 0 Yin

Trigrams: Earth comes into Wind

```
=====
== ==
== ==
```

When still, learn to create.
When in motion, learn stillness.
Know that circumstance mirrors inner growth.

4. Attunement

Mind: 10 Inquiry
Heart: 21 Becoming

Trigrams: Earth comes into Thunder

☷☳

Know that eternity is played by human beings.
The dance, the music, art: Know that is all there is.
Dance, make music and create art.

5. Opening

Mind: 10 Inquiry
Heart: 21 Becoming

Trigrams: Earth comes into Fire

☷☲

Open your heart to all wisdom, love and light.
Hold your heart opened, ready to be filled.
Follow the opportunity that leads to infinite possibility.

6. Alliance

Mind: 11 Growth
Heart: 21 Becoming

Trigrams: Earth comes into Stream

```
—  —
———
—  —
—  —
```

Focus your devotion and commitment.
Experience the growth gained in company.
Bond with others to strengthen the common center.

7. Patience

Mind: 11 Growth
Heart: 21 Becoming

Trigrams: Earth comes into Heaven

```
———
———
—  —
—  —
```

In adversity, give birth to patience.
Know patience as the mastery not of time, but of timing.
Pass the time by building bridges within.

8. Innocence

Mind: 20 Acquittal
Heart: 42 Being

Trigrams: Mountain comes into Earth

Become childlike.
Discern between truth and garbage.
Innocence is restored as garbage is let go.

9. Reflection

Mind: 20 Acquittal
Heart: 42 Being

Trigrams: Mountain comes into Mountain

Be still and know the Void.
Dwell beyond need and put your mind at rest.
Approach with awe the unmanifest field
that harbors all possibilities.

10. Inquiry

Mind: 21 Becoming
Heart: 42 Being

Trigrams: Mountain comes into Water

Be patient, accepting, flexible.
Know that blockage leads to breakthrough.
Know that complication leads to simplification.

11. Growth

Mind: 21 Becoming
Heart: 42 Being

Trigrams: Mountain comes into Wind

Sit back and enjoy the ride.
Be aware of the solid ground underneath.
Let conscious creation work with natural evolution.

12. Recognition

Mind: 30 Anticipation
Heart: 63 Yang

Trigrams: Mountain comes into Thunder

It is a time to observe in quietness.
If required, humbly respond with the simplest answers.
Approach within that which you want to re-cognize.

13. Fortuity

Mind: 30 Anticipation
Heart: 63 Yang

Trigrams: Mountain comes into Fire

In movement be settled; in wayfaring, centered.
Follow the blessed path of the butterfly.
Catch the cosmic wink.

14. Affinity

Mind: 31 Sustaining
Heart: 63 Yang

Trigrams: Mountain comes into Stream

☰

Reinforce belief with will and desire.
Temper action with humility and with vision.
Know that all relationships mirror yourself.

15. Equilibrium

Mind: 31 Sustaining
Heart: 63 Yang

Trigrams: Mountain comes into Heaven

☰

This is the time to let go.
Take time to rest in the shade.
Accept the dream of a new world
from the calm inner center.

16. Inclusion

Mind: 32 Beginning
Heart: 0 Yin

Trigrams: Water comes into Earth

```
— —   — —
— —   — —
———   — —
```

There *is* strength in numbers.
Strength may come from surprising sources.
Welcome compatible forces and widen your circle.

17. Questing

Mind: 32 Beginning
Heart: 0 Yin

Trigrams: Water comes into Mountain

```
— —   ———
— —   — —
———   — —
```

Be the beginner.
Settle into the role of the learner.
Know: It is the place most filled with opportunity.

18. Immersion

Mind: 33 Nourishment
Heart: 0 Yin

Trigrams: Water comes into Water

Hold out for consistency, integrity, clarity.
Heed the call that comes only to the strong of heart.
Go deep, keep aware and above all, keep heart.

19. Healing

Mind: 33 Nourishment
Heart: 0 Yin

Trigrams: Water comes into Wind

Gather the tools for transcendence.
There is medicine in moving on.
Both give and receive healing through service.

20. Acquittal

Mind: 42 Being
Heart: 21 Becoming

Trigrams: Water comes into Thunder

When the hook is withdrawn it is time to get off.
Seize the chance for change.
Breathe and move in the new freedom.

21. Becoming

Mind: 42 Being
Heart: 21 Becoming

Trigrams: Water comes into Fire

Who knows when the ripe apple will fall from the tree?
Or how the turning wheel will come to rest?
It is enough to feel the emerging rhythm.

22. Humility

Mind: 43 Wholeness
Heart: 21 Becoming

Trigrams: Water comes into Stream

Be the dolphin who gives in to the flood.
Sacrifice is essential if you would gain the truth.
Be truly humble: Live in a state of pure awe.

23. Pause

Mind: 43 Wholeness
Heart: 21 Becoming

Trigrams: Water comes into Heaven

Come into the safe center.
For balance and clarity, pause and take stock.
When it is time to act, do so only from the center.

24. Determination

Mind: 52 Repose
Heart: 42 Being

Trigrams: Wind comes into Earth

```
 --  --
 --  --
 ------
 --  --
```

Seek your purpose and fulfill your nature.
Be the flower that cracks open the rock that impedes it.
Be the persistent wind that changes the face of the earth.

25. Recovery

Mind: 52 Repose
Heart: 42 Being

Trigrams: Wind comes into Mountain

```
 --  --
 --  --
 ------
 --  --
```

Discern: Is it a matter of rebuilding?
Or simply letting what is outworn fall away?
Know that new worlds grow out of compost.

26. Honor

Mind: 53 Differentiation
Heart: 42 Being

Trigrams: Wind comes into Water

```
— — —
 ———
— — —
```

Remember that human nature, as all nature, is sacred.
Look for the natural changes in natural law.
The call to honor and compassion is unchanging.

27. Submission

Mind: 53 Differentiation
Heart: 42 Being

Trigrams: Wind comes into Wind

```
 ———
— — —
— — —
```

Give in and gain ground; power is already at work.
Detachment is especially important now.
Your natural influence is enough.

28. Constancy

Mind: 62 Change
Heart: 63 Yang

Trigrams: Wind comes into Thunder

Receive the gifts of detours and delays:
                                                            patience and growth.
Hold the center and the whole is centered.
Be in the moment and be in eternity.

29. Inspiration

Mind: 62 Change
Heart: 63 Yang

Trigrams: Wind comes into Fire

Be still; be inspired.
Keep centered, with an open mind, an open heart.
Know that inspiration seeks out the opened heart.

30. Anticipation

Mind: 63 Yang
Heart: 63 Yang

Trigrams: Wind comes into Stream

```
-- --
-----
-----
-- --
```

Anchor disquiet in the invisible center.
Know that the most active imagination creates in stillness.
Find meaning in this moment, not that past or that future.

31. Sustaining

Mind: 63 Yang
Heart: 63 Yang

Trigrams: Wind comes into Heaven

```
-----
-----
-----
-- --
```

Adjust your focus.
Tune to the beauty in the way things are.
Turn your power to appreciation of what already is.

32. Beginning

Mind: 0 Yin
Heart: 0 Yin

Trigrams: Thunder comes into Earth

```
_  _
_  _
_  _
_____
```

Know that the oak begins with the death of the acorn.
Feel the height reached only when the depth is plumbed.
Sense the turning as evolution becomes creation.

33. Nourishment

Mind: 0 Yin
Heart: 0 Yin

Trigrams: Thunder comes into Mountain

```
_____
_  _
_  _
```

Know that the mouth regulates both life and death.
Find balance with your appetites.
Find peace through speaking words
of comfort and compassion.

34. Birth

Mind: 1 Closure
Heart: 0 Yin

Trigrams: Thunder comes into Water

Cherish the offspring born out of great labor.
Know the child as the child reveals itself.
Recognize and nurture the gifts.

35. Compassion

Mind: 1 Closure
Heart: 0 Yin

Trigrams: Thunder comes into Wind

Be committed to the infinite worth of all,
beginning with yourself.
Feel the infinite generosity of the universe.
Heed the humblest need and hear the faintest cry,
starting with yourself.

36. Induction

Mind: 10 Inquiry
Heart: 21 Becoming

Trigrams: Thunder comes into Thunder

```
-- --
-----
-- --
-----
```

Sit calmly and feel both solace and power.
Find the treasure brought in by the storm.
Witness as the phoenix rises from the ash.

37. Endurance

Mind: 10 Inquiry
Heart: 21 Becoming

Trigrams: Thunder comes into Fire

```
-----
-- --
-----
-- --
```

Push on through to the finish.
Know that the journey and the destiny are one.
Persistence and hard work call for celebration.

38. Balance

Mind: 11 Growth
Heart: 21 Becoming

Trigrams: Thunder comes into Stream

Come to balance through quietness.
Feel balance come to light at the center.
Be quiet and relieve stress; allow inspiration and renewal.

39. Spontaneity

Mind: 11 Growth
Heart: 21 Becoming

Trigrams: Thunder comes into Heaven

Honor the mood.
Bring heaven to earth now.
Feel the movement of the spirit, which heeds its own time.

40. Paradox

Mind: 20 Acquittal
Heart: 42 Being

Trigrams: Fire comes into Earth

```
==  ==
==  ==
======
======
```

Initiate action, if any, only with utmost thoughtfulness.
React only in full accord with your principles and values.
In a storm, be at the calm heart.

41. Benediction

Mind: 20 Acquittal
Heart: 42 Being

Trigrams: Fire comes into Mountain

```
======
==  ==
==  ==
```

Find only serenity, beauty and grace.
Free yourself from judgment and expectation.
Know the greatest power: the benevolent spirit.

42. Being

Mind: 21 Becoming
Heart: 42 Being

Trigrams: Fire comes into Water

You have become, and now you are.
Know gain through loss, and loss through gain.
Be still and know yourself as you now are.

43. Wholeness

Mind: 21 Becoming
Heart: 42 Being

Trigrams: Fire comes into Wind

Remember the ancient greeting, "I Am Another Yourself."
Wear well your mask and honor the being inside.
Recognize the honored being inside others.

44. Epiphany

Mind: 30 Anticipation
Heart: 63 Yang

Trigrams: Fire comes into Thunder

Know that graduation is a passage, not an ending.
Be transformed by the moment that comes but once.
Carry from the mountaintop the supreme revelation.

45. Combustion

Mind: 30 Anticipation
Heart: 63 Yang

Trigrams: Fire comes into Fire

Feel yourself as the fire.
Know that fire is fueled by those who sacrifice.
Ignite with all loving care and compassion.

46. Momentum

Mind: 31 Sustaining
Heart: 63 Yang

Trigrams: Fire comes into Stream

With detachment and humor, abandon yourself to change.
Define and clarify the norms of the new.
Relax and unwind into the new.

47. Networking

Mind: 31 Sustaining
Heart: 63 Yang

Trigrams: Fire comes into Heaven

Bring unity and gain through common purpose.
Know the whole as the expansion of the center.
Nurture at your own center
the qualities you want in the world.

48. Awareness

Mind: 32 Beginning
Heart: 0 Yin

Trigrams: Stream comes into Earth

▤

Find the truth between emotion and intellect.
Feel personal power increase through honesty.
Be self-aware and turn fault into freedom.

49. Simplicity

Mind: 32 Beginning
Heart: 0 Yin

Trigrams: Stream comes into Mountain

▤

Know that which is loss to some is liberty to others.
Remember that true wealth can never be taken away.
Feel the greatest treasure: Gratitude within.

50. Definition

Mind: 33 Nourishment
Heart: 0 Yin

Trigrams: Stream comes into Water

Carve out your identity.
Carefully select your roles.
Set boundaries by which you can live.

51. Deepening

Mind: 33 Nourishment
Heart: 0 Yin

Trigrams: Stream comes into Wind

Learn from empathy.
Enter wisdom through the heart.
Be guided by intuition, the way into the heart.

52. Repose

Mind: 42 Being
Heart: 21 Becoming

Trigrams: Stream comes into Thunder

```
__ __
_____
__ __
_____
```

Give in.
Be motionless here, now.
Fold your wings and take a rest.

53. Differentiation

Mind: 42 Being
Heart: 21 Becoming

Trigrams: Stream comes into Fire

```
_____
__ __
_____
```

Meet others where they are.
Heed all issues, all points of view.
Define and clarify, and understanding will follow.

54. Devotion

Mind: 43 Wholeness
Heart: 21 Becoming

Trigrams: Stream comes into Stream

Awe and humor light the way.
Laughter restores the heart.
Partake of the joy you have earned.

55. Equality

Mind: 43 Wholeness
Heart: 21 Becoming

Trigrams: Stream comes into Heaven

Move with the spirit, with all honor and humility.
Feel the constancy of change.
Feel the assurance of inspiration.

56. Oneness

Mind: 52 Repose
Heart: 42 Being

Trigrams: Heaven comes into Earth

Earth positioned over heaven brings harmonious union.
Know yourself as others.
Know others as yourself.

57. Sensitivity

Mind: 52 Repose
Heart: 42 Being

Trigrams: Heaven comes into Mountain

Remember: Two eyes and two ears -- only one mouth.
Be sensitive to each slight influence.
Hear the song in every heartbeat, starting within.

58. Attention

Mind: 53 Differentiation
Heart: 42 Being

Trigrams: Heaven comes into Water

Be the stillness, centered in the midst of motion.
Feel stillness and motion meet in the breath.
Practice inhaling deeply, exhaling completely.

59. Expansion

Mind: 53 Differentiation
Heart: 42 Being

Trigrams: Heaven comes into Wind

It is time to learn to stretch.
Accept the distance as the gap widens.
Refocus your energies; the center holds.

60. Charisma

Mind: 62 Change
Heart: 63 Yang

Trigrams: Heaven comes into Thunder

Remember that the brightest light serves the most.
Know the seat of power as the seat of responsibility.
Bring light and power to balance between self and others.

61. Bounty

Mind: 62 Change
Heart: 63 Yang

Trigrams: Heaven comes into Fire

Be clear in the matter of values.
Know that heart and spirit cannot be measured.
Know that abundance cannot be put in the bank.

62. Change

Mind: 63 Yang
Heart: 63 Yang

Trigrams: Heaven comes into Stream

Yield to the momentum of change.
Delight in new discoveries.
Be open about your concerns, affirming the least heeded.

63. Yang

Mind: 63 Yang
Heart: 63 Yang

Trigrams: Heaven comes into Heaven

With great mercy, breathe life into the dream.
With great compassion, light up the dark cave.
Know: Creation begins with a seed and an impulse.

*A Brief Pre-Wen History
of the I Ching,
Elucidating
the Ancient Cryptogram*

*A*fter a perusal of all the available versions of the I Ching, a particular fact became evident: there appeared no clear history of the I Ching prior to King Wen's re-do of it in approximately 1100 b.c.e.; there were only sketchy, vague speculations from divergent viewpoints, with one single, notable exception.

Therefore, in *The Nu I Ching*, we will take a good look at what we can discover of the I Ching prior to the time of Wen's extensive revisions. This will take us back in time by approximately 5,000 years, some two millennia before King Wen.

In its beginning, the meaning of the *"I"* of I Ching was *"the simple, easy and naturally given."*, *Ching* simply means a book or a text. Hellmut Wilhelm *Eight Lectures on the I Ching* (Bollingen Series LXII, Princeton University, 1960) in which he calls the I Ching the "Book of Changes," by which title it is commonly known, told us (pp. 16-17):

> The first thing the literal meaning of the character "I" yields us is the easy, the simple, the naturally given. I would like to emphasize this point because it highlights the difference between the system of the Book of Changes in the version presented by the early Chou rulers and in preceding versions. We miss the meaning of this system if at the outset we look for something dark and mysterious in it. The book starts from what everyone sees and can immediately grasp...

> The situations depicted in the Book of Changes are the primary data of life, what happens to everybody every day, and what is simple and easy to understand...

> Again and again the emphasis is on simplicity and lucidity as the only gateway to this system. 'The good that lies in the easy and the simple' we read, 'makes it correspond to the highest kind of existence'..."

Figure 2
the original pictogram for the "I" of I Ching
("ching" simply means a book or a text)

While "ching" simply means a book or text, the original pictogram for the "I" of I Ching, shown in *Figure 2*, is an enigmatic figure which has come down to us as "the easy, the simple, the naturally given." A later meaning that was ascribed to the pictogram was that of "change," hence "Book of Changes," for Hellmut tells us:

> The character *I*, which in translation we have simplified as 'change'... The first meaning seems to have been 'lizard' (pp. 13-14, *Eight Lectures...*)

Certainly the general meaning of "change," typified by the chameleon, can be seen in this use of the term "lizard," and who indeed would argue the fact that change is the only unchangeable? Yet a mere glance at the figure leaves room for wide speculation, and for doubt as to the certitude of its "simplified translation" as *change*.

Dr. Martin Schönberger, who wrote *The I Ching & The Genetic Code* in 1973 (Aurora Press, Santa Fe, NM, 1992), convincingly argues that the symbol bears reference to nothing less than our genetic code, DNA. But before we turn our attention to that absorbing phenomenon, let's look at the time of Fu Hsi and Nu Kua, 5,000 years ago. *The Nu I Ching* attributes the original development of the I Ching as shown in the circular cryptogram, which we will explore, to both members of that couple rather than to just the male of the pair, taking its cue from Dr. Schönberger in his preface:

> Fu-Hsi and Nu-Kua (Niu-Koa) *"the first married couple"* (and at the same time brother and sister) stand at the dawn of history as it emerges from myth. They have mythical characteristics (dragon tails and wings) and also carry instruments of precision (set-square and compasses). Together these instruments betoken: "order and correct behavior."
>
> Never again in Chinese history do we find such a striking picture of a couple, where stress is laid on the equal excellence of the high cultural achievements of the two partners, which are recorded partly in the form of myths (Nu-Kua's deeds in restoring order to a world out of joint) and are partly of a historical character (Fu-Hsi as the inventor of a system of knot writing, of the eight trigrams and their arrangement, and also of agriculture and hunting; Nu-Kua as the "inventress" of matrimony with an account of her family clan, etc.) - indeed, the couple seem to be a representation of Tao itself in its appearance as yang and yin.

Figure 3 - Nu Kua and Fu Hsi
with compasses and set-square

We are fortunate that the classic stone rubbing shown in *Figure 3* has survived to illustrate this connection (identified as Nu Kua and Fu Hsi by Erwin Burckhardt, *Chinesische Steinabriebungen*, Hirmer Verlag, Munich, 1962, plate 1). According to Schönberger:

> Fu Hsi holds the set-square in his left hand. As it is used to draw the square, it represents an emblem of the earth, i.e., of the "female principle" (yin), and can hold good as the insignia of the male principle only after an exchange of attributes completed during hierogamy. Similarly Nu-Kua, his wife, carries the compasses, the circle-producing emblem of the sky, of the "male principle" (yang).

In the stone rubbing we can see the two with serpent tails entwined -- an unmistakable double helix design evocative of our DNA, which Schönberger has illuminated, showing the stunning correspondence of DNA to the patterning of the I Ching. As well, the Figure Eight – the "infinity" symbol – is prominently incorporated in the depiction of the joining of the two.

As stated in Schönberger's quote above, the set-square held by Fu Hsi represents the earth (Yin), and the compasses held by Nu Kua represent the heavens (Yang).

This leads us to the cryptogram, the 64 hexagrams arranged in a square situated within a circle of the 64, and to the single notable exception that is consistent from available pre-Wen history, the *ba gua* that is commonly attributed to Fu Hsi. Based on the stone rubbing shown in *Figure 3*, we include Nu Kua in their joint creative endeavors.

The *ba gua* consists of all possible combinations of Yin and Yang expressed in three lines. The trigrams are read as though one is standing in the center of the octagon and looking out. Yin is an open line, and Yang a solid line:

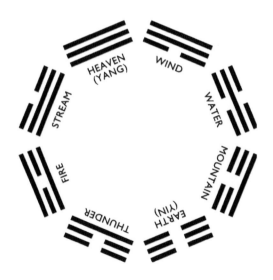

Figure 4 - the ba gua
the eight trigrams

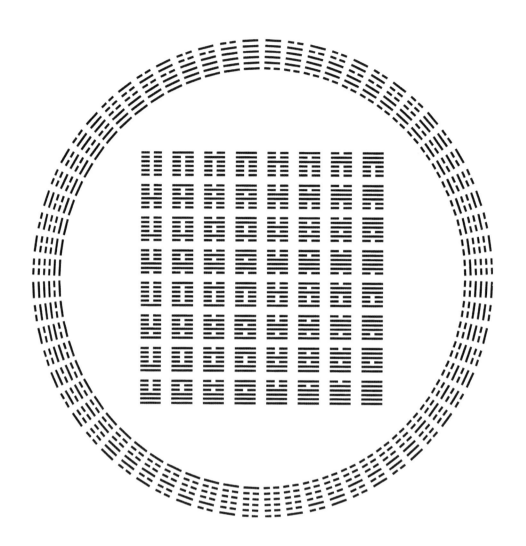

Figure 5
the ancient cryptogram --
the square representing the earth
situated within the circle of the heavens

This arrangement, like the tools shown in the stone rubbing -- where Nu Kua (Yin) holds the Yang compasses and Fu Hsi (Yang) holds the Yin set-square -- represents the earth and the heavens, the square of the earth balanced within the encircling framework of the heavens.

The cryptogram shown in *Figure 5* in popular I Ching histories is attributed to Shao Yung, or else to "a forgotten Sung scholar," circa 1000 a.d. – one mere millennium ago. In *DNA and the I Ching: The Tao of Life* (North Atlantic Books, Berkeley, CA, 1991), Johnson F. Yan states:

> The forgotten Sung scholar who discovered this arrangement probably thought it so natural and beautiful that he dared not claim credit for himself but instead credited it to the great Fu Hsi. This is not an unusual practice for ancient Chinese scholars, though it has just the opposite effect on modern Western ears than the humbling one intended: imagine a modern physicist crediting a good piece of his own work to Sir Isaac Newton!

Even the celebrated I Ching scholar Hellmut Wilhelm, in his *Eight Lectures on the I Ching* (p. 89), subscribed to the notion that such a perfect blueprint of the patterning of all human experience and behavior, encoded in the prehistoric cryptogram, could have sprung into place in Shao Yung's lifetime, a mere thousand years ago:

> Shao Yung's exactitude led him to work out a different I Ching table, in which he arranges the hexagrams in a natural system.

While Shao Yung earned renown as a master of the I Ching, it is doubtful that he himself would take credit for the double arrangement of the hexagrams in the cryptogram, and due to honesty, not modesty. Whether credit is given, as it is in most accounts, to Shao Yung, or to an unknown scholar of the same period, matters not in our context. We are looking at the time period, and proposing that rather than originating during the Sung period, when Shao Yung lived, the cryptogram in fact originated *at least* 4000 years earlier, with Nu Kua and Fu Hsi.

The cryptogram reveals a perfect ordering inherent in the system of the 64 hexagrams, at the same time simple and complex, an order that is reflected precisely in the arrangement of the *ba gua* (*Figure 4*). Just as no one can assemble a jigsaw puzzle into a picture without the puzzle having been a complete picture before it was cut into pieces, we do not see how anyone could have produced the cryptogram, with its precision and perfection, without its *original* innate perfect ordering. *The key lies in the dovetailing of the cryptogram with the Nu Kua/Fu Hsi ba gua, commonly known to have originated circa 3000 b.c.e.*

It follows that the assembly of the hexagrams credited to Shao Yung, or to an unknown scholar also from the Sung dynasty, circa 1000 a.d., was in actual fact a *reassembly*, a restoration to a former, prehistoric order. It was finally re-assembled during the Sung dynasty, over two thousand years after King Wen dismantled the ordering of the already ancient code, circa 1100 b.c.e., and imposed his own.

Figure 6 shows the *ba gua* positioned with the cryptogram, both the square and the circle, revealing the perfect overlay that results. The eight trigrams of the *ba gua* are superimposed for illustrative purposes on the square in the positions where a trigram is repeated in both the upper and lower positions of a given hexagram. This placement results in a precise consecutive diagonal formation. On the circle, the placement of the *ba gua* coincides perfectly with the occurrence of the hexagrams in which the respective upper and lower trigrams are repeated, as with the square:

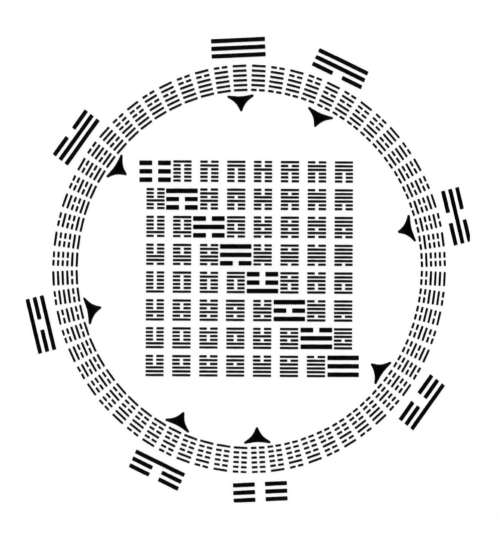

Figure 6
the ba gua naturally synchronized with the cryptogram
indicating a common origin of the two

On the circle, both the *ba gua* and the circular pattern of the 64 hexagrams begin at the bottom with Yin (0) and ascend counterclockwise through four trigrams (on the *ba gua*) and 32 hexagrams (on the cryptogram). Then the flow descends, proceeding clockwise to Yang (63), flowing again to Yin in a "lemniscate," the *infinity symbol*, to continue in its endless circuits.

The syncopation at the top and bottom of the circle in *Figure 6* leads us to the next step in our exploration of the cryptogram, when we will find that precise sequences of eight hexagrams flow between those of the *ba gua*. The cluster of four hexagrams at the top continues at the bottom with the next four, totaling eight. On the square, reading across the rows from top left to bottom right we find that, as with the circle, precise sequences of eight hexagrams flow between those of the *ba gua*. The exception, on both the square and the circle, is that Yang flows directly to Yin.

In *Figure 7*, the red arrows trace the Yin hemisphere (to the right on the diagram), while the blue arrows trace the Yang hemisphere (to the left on the diagram). The two, Yin and Yang, hold together the entire system in a dynamic ever-moving flux, Yin at the root and foundation, the earth, and Yang at the peak and zenith, the heavens, together completing the two loops of infinity.

Yin (0) comes before all and must exist before anything can emerge, for as the *zero*, she precedes all numbers and contains all potential. Yin is the pregnant void that harbors all possibilities.

The word *zero* originally meant "empty." Yin represents emptiness as the womb is empty, as the soil before it is seeded. No human being can enter life without the womb, or be fed without the soil. Yang (63) comes last among the 64 hexagrams, and is the culmination, the completion, of the work of creation and evolution.

Figure 7
circular cryptogram and ba gua showing the dynamic
flow between the Yin and Yang hemispheres

You may notice the visual similarity of *Figure 7* to the bicameral structure of the brain, its right and left hemispheres, with their differing, complementary and inter-dependent functions, just as there is a direct correspondence between Yin and Yang functions.

On the circle, the first line of all the hexagrams in the Yin hemisphere, and the first line of all the trigrams in the Yin hemisphere of the *ba gua* – the line closest to the center of the circle – is a Yin line, an open line. Meanwhile, the first line of each hexagram in the Yang hemisphere, and of each trigram in the Yang hemisphere in the *ba gua*, is a Yang line, a solid line. This is graphically illustrated in *Figure 1*, the ancient depiction of the 64 hexagrams reproduced at the beginning of this book.

The array in *Figure 8* further illustrates the interconnectedness and balance within the system. The Yin and Yang hemispheres are mirrored from right to left, the distinction between the two hemispheres indicated by a heavy dotted line.

The center circle of numbers consists only of the four Innermost (Heart) hexagrams – Yin (0), Becoming (21), Being (42), and Yang (63), mirrored exactly left to right.

Raying from these four are the sixteen Inner (Mind) hexagrams, shown in the middle ring of numbers. These, like the Heart hexagrams, are exactly mirrored left to right.

The Mind hexagrams in turn radiate outward to the full array of the 64 Outer hexagrams. Only these 64 do not mirror themselves, rather there are complementary correspondences.

The hexagrams are tinted: Yin is red, for soil and for blood, the seat of human life. Becoming is yellow, as the sun rises and brings new becoming, new unfolding. Being is green for manifest growth in nature, and Yang is blue for the encircling heavens.

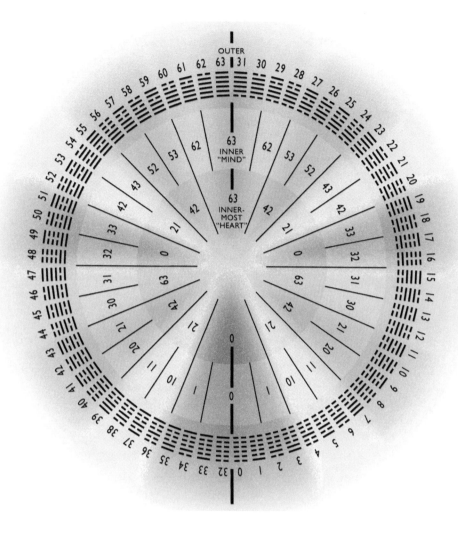

Figure 8
depicting the perfection of the system
with the Mind and Heart hexagrams nestled within the 64
and applying color
red for Yin (Earth), yellow for Becoming,
green for Being, blue for Yang (Heaven)

The symmetries and syntheses of the system are mind-boggling, and one begins to understand why the Jesuits, who centuries ago discovered the I Ching in China, are said to have gone insane. In their case, it confounded completely the world view they represented, with the result that its study was banned. After some fifteen years of avocational study, my own awe at the unfolding richness increases.

Here we have touched on the mirror-imaging of the hexagrams. Look again at the ancient depiction of the 64 hexagrams shown at the beginning of this book, *Figure 1*. In this depiction, the correspondence to the circle of the cryptogram is exact, with white squares where there are Yin lines and black squares where there are Yang lines. If turned the other way, the colors would be reversed.

When *Figure 1* is folded right to left, as with the cryptogram, all squares mirror themselves except the first row, nearest the center, where alone Yin and Yang mirror each other. However, when folded horizontally, up and down, the opposite is true: all hexagrams meet their complement – Yin to Yang – except at the first row, nearest the center, where Yin and Yang each mirror themselves.

The *zero* of Yin in the I Ching is the earth; on a greater scale Yin corresponds to the mystery and the completeness of Nuit, who is all of space, and within whom all emanates. Yang in the I Ching is the evident heavens, on a greater scale corresponding to the motion of Hadit, as the stars in the night sky. (In turn -- though not our focus here -- Ra-Hoor-Khuit represents the experiences and shifts of human life encoded within the oracle.)

In *The Mother's Agenda*, Mira Alfassa said, "I had a vision of a kind of infinite Eternity through which the Supreme Consciousness voyages..." In this vision, Nuit, or Yin, would be representative of the "infinite Eternity," and Hadit, or Yang, of the motion of "Supreme Consciousness."

The ancients stood on the earth (Yin) and looked into the heavens (Yang), and saw that the positions of the two stayed the same. Heaven was always above, and Earth was always beneath. In our day, having viewed Earth from space, we can envision the South Pole and the North Pole as Yin and Yang, perpetually defining the two poles of our experience in this world, on this planet, together embracing and holding the whole of it, staying in their mutually complementary positions, yet remaining apart, so that we can experience our existence.

Let's turn now to the Heart and Mind hexagrams and see how they are embedded within a given hexagram. We simply remove the top and bottom lines; the remaining four lines become the Inner or Mind hexagram. Then as the top and bottom lines of this new hexagram are removed, the Innermost or Heart hexagram emerges. Each time a pair of lines is removed, the number of possible combinations is diminished, so that there are only sixteen possible "Mind" hexagrams and only four possible "Heart" hexagrams.

Another way to arrive at the Heart hexagram is by creating a lower trigram from lines 2, 3, and 4, and an upper trigram from lines 3, 4, and 5 of the original hexagram. The bottom two and top two lines are the Mind hexagram. Repeat this process with the new hexagram. You will have one of only four hexagrams: Yin (six Yin lines), Becoming (alternating lines beginning with Yin), Being (alternating lines beginning with Yang), or Yang (six Yang lines). As further inner hexagrams are calculated, Yin produces Yin and Yang produces Yang, while Being and Becoming endlessly alternate.

We can see that the ancients could observe Heaven as always up and Earth as always down, their relative positions stationary, as Yin and Yang each remain. But the ancients could turn around, where left and right change places, one turning into the other just like the hexagrams, where Becoming turns into Being and Being turns into Becoming.

Similarly, the North and South Poles remain up and down by our orientation. And as we look from space – and perhaps the ancients did too in some way unknown to most of us – we can see that while the poles remain in their north and south positions, the equator turns, day turning into night and night turning into day. Such is the nature of Yin and Yang, which remain Yin and Yang, and of Being and Becoming, which endlessly alternate, as we go deeper into each of the 64 hexagrams and calculate further the embedded hexagrams.

It is not necessary to have separate sections for the four Heart and sixteen Mind hexagrams as we have done in *The Nu I Ching*. One can derive a complete three-tiered reading by determining the Mind and Heart levels and simply reading those as they occur among the 64.

It is quite possible that the depiction of the hexagrams shown in *Figure 1* is older than the cryptogram shown in *Figure 5*, which itself is prehistoric, considering the fact that the era of origin of the latter has been heretofore unknown, rather, it is still popularly thought to have originated as recently as one thousand years ago, a period which we believe to be evidently in serious doubt for reasons presented in this book.

In *Figure 9*, the six-pointed star emerges when we pinpoint the Mind and Heart hexagrams as they are numerically situated among the 64. The single asterisks indicate the sixteen Mind hexagrams, and the double asterisks show the placement of the four Heart hexagrams, which occur among the sixteen. As with the *ba gua* overlay, between each set of Inner and Innermost hexagrams, there are eight hexagrams.

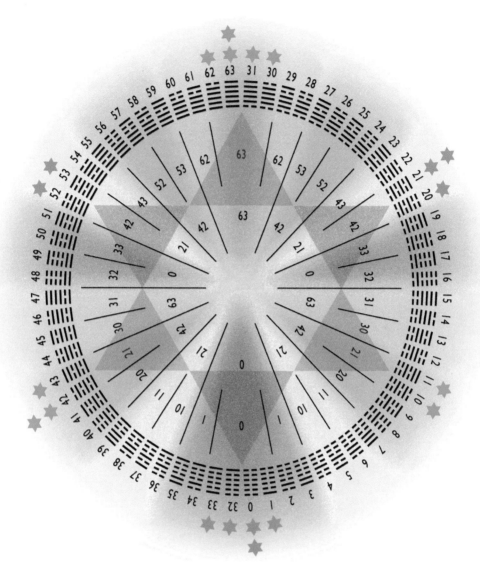

Figure 9
a six-pointed star results when we show
the placement of the sixteen Mind hexagrams
and the four Heart hexagrams among the 64
with eight hexagrams appearing between each set

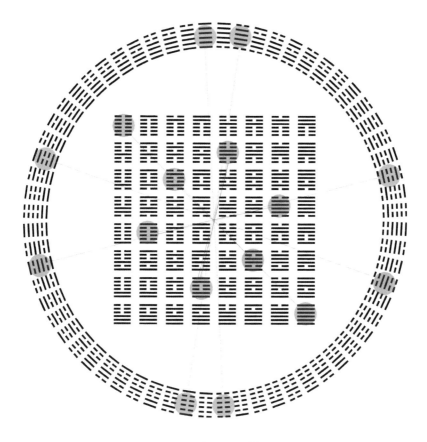

Figure 10
showing the eight reversible hexagrams
paired with their complements

Figure 10 shows the eight hexagrams that remain unchanged when turned upside-down, each paired with its complement, Yin lines to Yang, and Yang lines to Yin. Those with Yin at the heart are shown in red, those with Yang at the heart in blue.

If the square is folded diagonally, top right corner to bottom left corner, the tinted upper and lower trigrams are reversed. Folded top left to bottom right corner, the tinted trigrams complete each other.

Focusing now on the square in the cryptogram, we read across the *lines* of the hexagrams, starting with Yin at the top left corner and ending with Yang at bottom right. When all six lines have been read, we find:

<u>Line 6</u>: *One* Yin line is followed by *one* Yang line.
<u>Line 5</u>: *Two* Yin lines are followed by *two* Yang lines.
<u>Line 4</u>: *Four* Yin lines are followed by *four* Yang lines.
<u>Line 3</u>: *Eight* Yin lines are followed by *eight* Yang lines.
<u>Line 2</u>: *Sixteen* Yin lines are followed by *16* Yang lines.
<u>Line 1</u>: *Thirty-two* Yin lines are followed by *32* Yang lines.

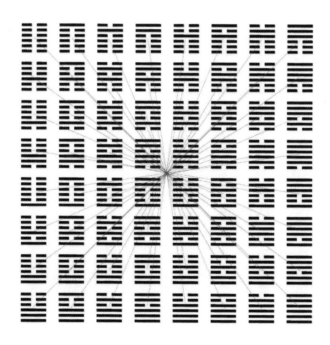

Figure 11
the square in the cryptogram also showing
complementary hexagrams, where all Yin lines are
paired with Yang lines as indicated by connecting lines

Next we will apply color to show the locations of other primary hexagrams as they occur on the square, thus expanding on the symmetry:

The <u>Yin and Yang</u> hexagrams are outlined in blue.
The <u>four Innermost (Heart)</u> hexagrams are outlined in red.
The <u>8 *Trigrams* (the *ba gua)*</u> are outlined in green.
The <u>16 Inner (Mind)</u> hexagrams are shaded with purple.

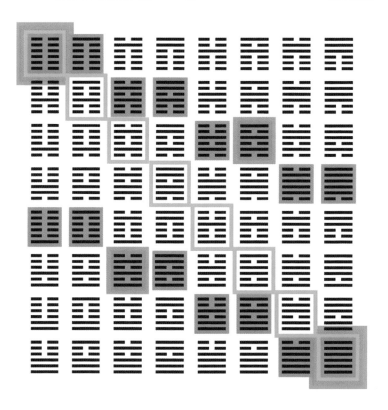

Figure 12
the square in the cryptogram
with primary hexagrams indicated by color

Below, the square of the 64 is reproduced in order to show the symmetry that occurs in the placement of the Heart hexagrams. The corresponding numbers replace the actual hexagrams. Repeating the emphases from *Figure 12*, the diagonal *ba gua* are marked with double asterisks **, Inner hexagrams with **bold face and underlining**. The pound sign (#) indicates the Innermost hexagrams.

In the ancient cryptogram the hexagrams are naturally arranged according to their Innermost, or Heart lines. To illustrate this, tints are applied, using the same code as that of the circle: Yin, Becoming, Being, Yang.

**#0	I	2	3	4	5	6	7
8	**9	10	I I	12	13	I 4	I 5
16	17	**18	19	**20**	#21	22	23
24	25	26	**27	28	29	**30**	**31**
32	**33	34	35	**36	37	38	39
40	41	#42	**43**	44	**45	46	47
48	49	50	51	**52**	**53**	**54	55
56	57	58	59	60	61	**62**	**#63

Figure 13
the square with hexagrams replaced by their numbers
showing the locations of the respective Heart hexagrams

The following tables show more numerical symmetry.

The hexagrams are identified by their Heart hexagrams as referenced from *Figure 13*.

The sums and Inner (Mind) hexagrams and the numerical resolutions are shown in bold type and italics.

Innermost (Heart) hexagrams are noted by the # sign. The *ba gua* is referenced by * asterisks.

- The totals of all rows increase by *64* – the total number of hexagrams – as do the sums.

- The columns increase by *sixteen* – the number of the Inner hexagrams.

- The sums of the columns increase by *four* – the number of the Innermost hexagrams.

- Yin's primary hexagrams include both the elements Earth and Water as represented in the *ba gua* (0 and 18) and Yin is devoid of Fire and Heaven. In turn, Yang shows Fire and Heaven (45 and 63) and is devoid of Earth and Water.

- Becoming contains the trigrams Thunder and Stream (36 and 54) and is devoid of Mountain and Wind, while Being contains Mountain and Wind (9 and 27) and is devoid of Thunder and Stream.

- The tables resolve in consecutive order to 3, 4, 5, 6, which total nine. Likewise, each hexagram represented in the *ba gua*, save 0, totals 9: 9, 18, 27, 36, 45, 54, and 63. Nine is a key number in the I Ching, as the intervals of eight hexagrams between primary hexagrams lead to the ninth in a rhythmic sequence.

YIN (0):

*#0	1	2	3	=	6	=	6
16	17	*18	19	=	70	=	7
32	33	34	35	=	134	=	8
48	49	50	51	=	198	=	9
96	100	104	108	=	408	=	3

BECOMING (21):

4	5	6	7	=	22	=	4
20	#21	22	23	=	86	=	5
*36	37	38	39	=	150	=	6
52	53	*54	55	=	214	=	7
112	116	120	124	=	472	=	4

BEING (42):

8	* 9	10	11	=	38	=	2
24	25	26	*27	=	102	=	3
40	41	#42	43	=	166	=	4
56	57	58	59	=	230	=	5
128	132	136	140	=	536	=	5

YANG (63):

12	13	14	15	=	54	=	9
28	29	30	31	=	118	=	10
44	*45	46	47	=	182	=	11
60	61	62	*#63	=	246	=	12
144	148	152	156	=	600	=	6

Figure 14 – Heart-based tables of the square

The four Heart hexagrams consist of all possible Yin and Yang bigrams, as the *ba gua* consists of all possible combinations of Yin and Yang when expressed in three lines, and the 64 hexagrams consist of all possible arrangements of these eight trigrams when paired.

The trigrams consist of the four elements, which appear at the cardinal points *(Figure 4)*: Earth (0), Water (18), Fire (45) and Air (63). These manifest respectively, as Mountain (9), Stream (54), Thunder (36), Wind (27).

Earth is Yin (0); Air is Yang (63); their trigrams combined occur at the other two corners of the square (7 and 56). Water and Fire with their alternating Yin and Yang lines comprise Becoming and Being. In turn, these four hexagrams – Water (18), Becoming (21), Being (42), and Fire (45) – form a square within the square:

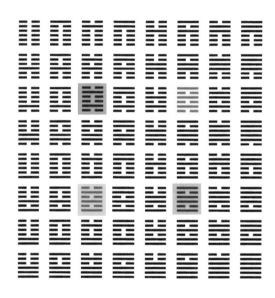

Figure 15
The hexagrams for Water, Becoming, Being, and Fire
form a square within the square

What Happened
to the I Ching
in King Wen's Time?

W hen Sharon Brown, Barbara Murray and I wrote the *Yin Book of Change* in 1995, under the pseudonym that combined our last names, Murray Ray Brown, we used Wen's numbering system, because that was all we knew. And we credited Shao Yung with originating the crypto-gram. We acknowledged previous scholars of the I Ching, "...and Shao Yung, whose thousand-year-old circular ar-rangement of the hexagrams we use, and most notably ... Richard Wilhelm, who gave us the news in 1929 that Yin came first." In Wen's system of the 64 hexagrams, Yang is number 1 and Yin is number 2.

From Richard Wilhelm, (*A Short History of Chinese Civilization*, NY Viking Press, 1929, p. 116):

> The extant collection of sixty-four diagrams, which began with the figure k'un ('the receptive') was certainly rearranged at the beginning of the Chou period. The text contains a number of passages which indicate the transition period between the two dynasties.

"K'un ('the receptive')" is Yin. While Richard brought the I Ching to the West, his son Hellmut Wilhelm popularized it in the West with his classic version of the I Ching. Hellmut tells us (*Eight Lectures on the I Ching*, p. 11):

> The reversal of the positions of the first two hexagrams, giving the father predominance over the mother, clearly carries the imprint of the patriarchal Chou dynasty.

So, based on the authority of both of the esteemed Wilhelm's, which had been ignored by the authors of all the oracles we found, daringly, we switched the first two hexagrams, making Yin number 1 and Yang number 2. But we retained all the rest of Wen's numbering system.

Yet even then, while we tried to combine the standardized Wen system with the obscure cryptogram, which, *sans* numbering or elucidation, Hellmut Wilhelm had included in his *Eight Lectures on the I Ching,* and José Arguelles had put in *The Mayan Factor* (Bear & Co., 1987), it seems now that the symmetry was trying to show itself all along. This is evidenced in the frontispiece that we printed in the *Yin Book of Change*, which is here reproduced *(Figure 17)* in order to show the cryptogram with Wen's numbers superimposed. We thought we were superimposing the symmetrical lines onto his system, which we accepted as the true gospel of the I Ching -- the gospel according to King Wen.

The square also demonstrates an incongruous ordering, for when we apply all 64 of Wen's numbers to the square of the cryptogram, this is what we get:

2	23	8	20	16	35	45	12
15	52	39	53	62	56	31	33
7	4	29	59	40	64	47	6
46	18	48	57	32	50	28	44
24	27	3	42	51	21	17	25
36	22	63	37	55	30	49	13
19	41	60	61	54	38	58	10
11	26	5	9	34	14	43	1

Figure 16
Wen's numbering system
applied to the square of the cryptogram

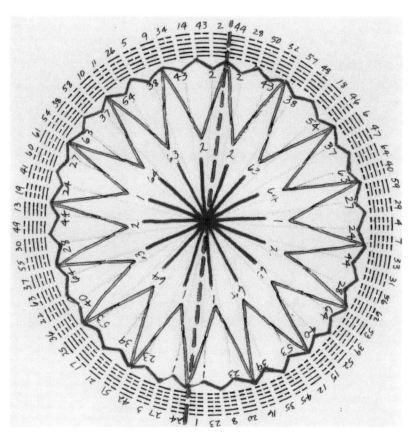

Figure 17
reproduced from the Yin Book of Change
showing an attempt at illustrating the symmetry
while using Wen's numbering system
(with numbers 1 and 2 reversed) ~
the red lines show the four Innermost hexagrams paired
with their complements -
yellow lines show the pairing of the Inner hexagrams -
the purple brackets indicate the binary placement
of the Innermost hexagrams - and the pink brackets
indicate the binary placement of the sixteen Inner
hexagrams as they flow to the pairs of Outer hexagrams

Figure 17 is reproduced here to show the incongruity of Wen's numbering system, which is copied unchanged except for the reversal of his numbers 1 and 2, Yin and Yang. The design symmetry was discovered through, and based entirely upon, the ordering of the hexagrams themselves, not on the imposed numbers, which only served to confuse. Uncounted futile hours were spent trying to make sense of the symmetry while maintaining Wen's numbers. And so, inevitably, something eluded us in our research.

So once our project was completed I continued. In 1998 I wrote the *Ladybug I Ching*, advancing the system but still using Wen's revision of the ordering, only sensing an underlying body of greater wisdom that glimmered tantalizingly through the veils. It was not until I finally experimented with the heresy of discarding Wen's system altogether that the antecedent order burst forth in clarity. The revision seems now like an undoing of the system.

The difference between the Wen system and the "easy, simple, naturally given" becomes clear when the Inner and Innermost hexagrams are allowed to emerge without his overlay, and without the embellishment of his son's "moving lines," wherein a "moving" hexagram sometimes appended to the thrown hexagram projects the reader into a nonexistent future. In the original system, the Inner and Innermost lines move naturally within all thrown hexagrams, disclosing the mind and heart of the matter, which are the forces at work at the time of the reading, advancing the reader's self-awareness and illuminating the inner as well as the outer experience.

So what was it that really happened to the I Ching around 1100 b.c.e.? As we have seen from both Wilhelms' quotes (page 88), Yang was given dominance over Yin, which until then came first.

When the receptive is put before the creative, the

creative has a matrix within which to manifest, in which to move and create -- as Mira Alfassa said, "I had a vision of a kind of infinite Eternity through which the Supreme Consciousness voyages." But when the creative is put before the receptive, through what will that Supreme Consciousness move? Where will the seed be planted? There will not yet be a ground, a womb, a space for it.

Richard Wilhelm went on to write (ibid, p. 85):

> The Book of Changes in the Yin period was not yet, however, the work now known by that name, but probably consisted of only sixty-four hexagrams, each of which had but one name.

It was only in the Chou dynasty, circa 1100 b.c.e., that "change" was ascribed to the pictogram for the *"I"* of I Ching (*Figure 2*), which until then denoted "the easy, the simple, the naturally given."

One might say in answer to the above quote that the I Ching currently consists of only 64 hexagrams, as indeed it does. With "but one name," however, he is inferring the hexagram upon which a reading is based, before the second hexagram – consisting of the "moving lines" – is imposed.

> According to general tradition, which we have no reason to challenge, the present collection of sixty-four hexagrams originated with King Wen, progenitor of the Chou dynasty. He is said to have added brief judgments to the hexagrams during his imprisonment at the hands of the tyrant Chou Hsin. The text pertaining to the individual lines originated with his son, the Duke of Chou.

The above quote is taken from the *Introduction to the I Ching*, HTML, ed. By Dan Baruth, 1999-2002. It is an accurate representation of conventional wisdom concerning the origin of the I Ching. In this quotation, the "text pertaining to the individual lines" -- the lines that move -- refers to the addition by Wen's son of the moving lines, which are still used in every available I Ching text.

From Hellmut Wilhelm, Richard's son, (ibid, p. 15):

> This word *I*, then, has given the name to the book which was arranged and enlarged from existing materials by King Wen at the end of the Shang period, about 1150 b.c. The material he found to hand did not yet bear the name *I*; the new arrangement devised by him was the first to be given this name. We have become accustomed to calling the book the I Ching, but *ching* is not an old word..."

So while King Wen renumbered the hexagrams, replacing the perfect symmetry with his own linear style, the text at that time also became the "Book of Change," in order to accommodate the "moving lines" added by Wen's son, the Duke of Chou. Richard Wilhelm is quoted above, "The Book of Changes in the Yin period was not yet...the work now known by that name." The "naturally given" Inner and Innermost hexagrams, advancing inner, spiritual, egalitarian values were obscured in favor of the patriarchal, hierarchical, external values then overtaking many of the world's cultures.

Serious scholars of the I Ching still defer to the Wen system, which for 3000 years now has eclipsed the flawless order, simplicity and symmetry of the Nu Kua/Fu Hsi system. Master Alfred Huang, one of Wen's most impressive proponents in our day, tells us in *The Numerology of the I Ching* (Inner Traditions, Rochester, VT, 2000, pp. 57-58):

> Most Western I Ching scholars believe the textual

sequence of King Wen's arrangement of the sixty-four gua is random. There seems to be no sound ground or reason to arrange the gua in such an order.

Huang goes on to offer his own explanation for the numerous "hidden" reasons for Wen's system of numbering, indeed, the chapter is titled "The Mysteries of King Wen's Sequence," denoting a purpose diametrically opposed to the original intent of the oracle, that of ease, simplicity, "what happens to everybody every day." As we have quoted Hellmut Wilhelm, "We miss the meaning of this system if at the outset we look for something dark and mysterious in it."

Huang tells us, "When King Wen rearranged the sequence of I to the present sequence of the sixty-four gua, it was not at random... it was based upon King Wen's political experience as well as his life philosophy..." Huang then explains that when Wen made Yang number one and Yin number two, it was because "the female horse should be submissive and responsive to the male horse's initiative. This is the Law of Nature, the Law of Heaven and Earth, and the Law of Humanity." Thus, according to Huang, Wen made his own political experience and life philosophy the "Law of Nature ... Heaven and Earth, and ... Humanity."

This mindset fomented the gender-based oppressions typified by the cruel and crippling custom of foot binding for Chinese females, which involved actually breaking the bones in the arch of the foot. Even in our new millennium we find published statements such as the following by Melyan & Chu in *I Ching, The Perfect Companion* (Black Dog & Leventhal Pub., NY, 2003, p. 15):

> The lines are of two kinds: the broken, representing the yin force, and the solid, representing the yang force.

The yin force refers to the negative, passive, weak, and destructive. It is docile and female. The yang force refers to the positive, active, strong, and constructive. It is virile and male.

In the above quoted book, there is no explanation as to how the passive, weak, and docile can also be the only destructive force. No wonder the receptive, open Yin line is traditionally labeled "broken."

How did it happen? How did such perfection and balance as found in the original pre-Wen system get lost? How was it replaced by a chaotic, fragmented, unbalanced system, while at the same time providing solace and guidance to untold multitudes throughout the centuries? Perhaps the solace and guidance is inherent in the system and reached the seekers, myself included, in spite of, not because of, the imposed misdirection.

But let us not be too hard on King Wen. For it was while he was imprisoned by the tyrant Chou Hsin that he made his rearrangement, applying his idea of social order to the meanings of the hexagrams, which up to that time reflected perfect balance between Yin and Yang, balance between Heaven and Earth, between male and female, between being and becoming.

Or perhaps it was not his idea at all. It is entirely possible that, due to the political intrigues and tyrannies of the day, and since Wen in prison was at the mercy of the tyrants, his ordering was coerced at pain of torture and even death. Indeed by extension his system imposes a tyranny of Yang over Yin, as attested and espoused by Huang, and by Melyan & Chu, although I believe that these contemporary scholars are doing their best to interpret and honor the system as they have come to know it.

Or maybe Wen's ordering was a gloss that he himself devised in order to satisfy his captors and tormentors. For

Wen knew that the authentic system which he rearranged was still extant. He may have done what he did with the I Ching while nurturing the hope that his gloss would be discarded and the real system restored to popular usage as soon as the tyrants fell. He may have believed that his system would coexist with the prior perfect system and to some degree people could take their pick despite the ruling tyrannical order.

For Wen could not have known what Emperor Chin, Han dynasty, would do some 900 years later, in 221 b.c.e. Obsessed with obtaining immortality, Chin finished the Great Wall of China, then set out to destroy the ancient documents. In the process he buried alive 240 scholars and burned all the books he could.

It is logical to surmise that Chin preserved the Wen I Ching system, since it is still widely extant, because it suited his idea of societal structure. Meanwhile he destroyed anything antecedent which he found in contradiction to his own purposes and designs. Such action would have led to the disappearance of the cryptogram, along with the suppression of the superior, flawless Nu Kua/Fu Hsi system.

The cryptogram eventually emerged from obscurity in Shao Yung's time, without numbering or naming. Swayed by the age-old monopoly of the Wen system, no one knew what to do with the cryptogram, other than credit the discoverer with having invented it.

So here we are, three millennia after Wen, two after Chin, and one after Shao Yung, still using the gloss. Was it Wen's own idea of social ordering, or an overlay he imposed to placate a ruling elite? Will we ever know?

What else can be said? We think it is time to uncover the subterfuge, and in so doing, restore the ease, simplicity, and "naturally given" perfection of the system.   ⊙

Epilogue

I am not a scientist, only a sporadic researcher when a topic captures my interest. I am fascinated by the exact correspondence of our DNA codons to the patterning of the I Ching, but all I can offer in this highly specialized area is a little repetition of what others have uncovered, a suggested correspondence to the cryptogram as elucidated in *The Nu I Ching*, and a hope that others will be stimulated to further the research that will illumine the transcendent wisdom of the ancients and collapse the time and culture barrier.

In his *I Ching and the Genetic Code*, Dr. Schönberger has elaborated on the ancient pictogram shown in *Figure 2*, page 64, effectively demonstrating that the ancients (who first offered it as "the easy, the simple, the naturally given" – H. Wilhelm) also based it on our genetic code. If we look at the modern graphic of the DNA double helix, we see how the ancient adepts made the connection, for we find that their imagery is a prehistoric template encrypting nothing less than our genetic code, our DNA.

But we do not have to rely merely on this image to discover a correspondence between the I Ching and the basic building blocks of life. Let's look again at the numbers. The formulating equation, $2 \times 2 = 4 \times 4 = 16 \times 4 = 64$, applies to both systems. We start with two lines, Yin and Yang. Arranging these two lines in all possible ways, we have the four Innermost hexagrams. From these four come the Inner hexagrams, of which there are only sixteen, and from these sixteen come the 64.

According to Johnson Yan *(DNA and the I Ching: The Tao of Life*, North Atlantic Books, Berkeley, CA, 1991), both DNA and the I Ching are based upon a code that generates a system of 64 possibilities compounded from its binary-quaternary properties. Both systems are embedded with specific principles that determine reliably predictable results – the response of the oracle in the I Ching, and the reaction of the amino acid in the DNA. And "both systems involve processes of transformation and change: in the I Ching, hexagrams change into other hexagrams; in DNA, point mutations occur through changes in the nucleotide bases." (The reference to hexagrams that "change into other hexa-grams," in our view, refers to the smooth, sinuous, deepening process provided by the flow among the Outer, Inner, and Innermost hexagrams.)

The four DNA designations, c-t-a-g, correspond to the Innermost hexagrams, their various combinations to the sixteen Inner hexagrams (4x4), and their triplet combinations to the organization of the bigrams and trigrams. Bernhard Pfennigschmidt has done some admirable work developing the correspondences between the I Ching and DNA. He acknowledges the correctness of our reading of the circle, from the inside, while showing the hexagrams as though the circle is read from the outside. He proposes a dual process, which fits with our use of the Heart and Mind hexagrams: "...the cosmos builds the template top/down. Humans asking for the oracle build it from the bottom up. That way interaction happens. The two extremes dilute until they meet in the middle." It was he who corrected my own numbering system, persuading me that Yin is 0 and Yang is 63, rather than Yin being 1 and Yang 64.

There is a world of room for study and discovery – receptivity and creativity – in this newly tantalizing field. What could possibly define DNA and describe its effects better than "the primary data of life, what happens to everybody every day"? (H. Wilhelm, *Eight Lectures,...* p. 17) *"...the easy, the simple, the naturally given..."*

For strictly illustrative purposes, if the rows of the square as shown in *Figure 13*, page 83, were freed, the double helix in *Figure 18* below might appear. The rows with Yin and Becoming (1, 3, 5, 7) would emerge as the red and yellow strand, and the rows with Being and Yang (2, 4, 6, 8) as the blue and green strand.

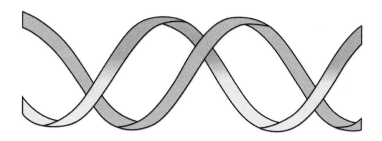

Figure 18
the square freed to show its DNA correspondence

If we extend the graphic illustration to the circle, as depicted in *Figures 7-9*, pages 73-79, we might see a design similar to that shown below, wherein the four colors are combined in both strands:

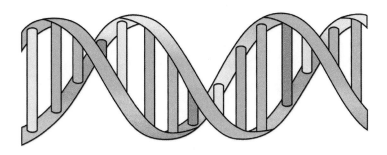

Figure 19
the circle dancing to show its DNA correspondence

Other books from ARay Press:

Fables by the Sea
Ode to Earth in 9-11 Meter
Pathways with Geoisms
Prisms and Songs for the Beloved
Return of the Prodigal Genius
The Forest Dweller
The Stickspeaker Collection
Wings of Comfort